Encounters
One Word Devotions

Billie Keeling Carroll

Purpose Publishing

ISBN:1-7337729-0-1
ISBN-13:978-1-7337729-0-7

This book is dedicated to my husband and life partner, Ron. To my two sons, Tommy and Todd, and two beautiful granddaughters, Madison and Morgan. They are all so precious to me, and precious in God's sight.

To my parents, Pastors W. T. and Lillian Keeling, who raised me in church and raised me to love and serve the Lord. I am so thankful for my heritage and the legacy they left for all our family.

To my pastors, Sam and Becky Carr, who have loved and prayed for us. Not only are they our pastors, but our friends for over 20 years.

To my many friends who have encouraged and motivated me to do this. Thank you so much for your friendship and inspiration. I pray the blessings and supernatural favor of God be upon your lives. You are all treasures to me. I value and appreciate every one of you!

INTRODUCTION

We often wish God would speak to us the way He spoke to His people in biblical times – through a burning bush, through a dove descending from the sky, or through the parting of a body of water so we can cross to the other side of our challenging situations. God's way of speaking to us doesn't have to be complicated. As a matter of fact, He often speaks to us in simple ways with simple truths. God often speaks to me with just a single word during my prayer or worship time. When He gives me a word, I look up the definition and see what the scriptures have to say about it. This devotional is a combination of one-word inspirations and testimonies of some of my life's experiences. We all at times need encouragement, motivation to press on and to move forward. Sometimes a little push is all we need and just one word from God can do the trick. My prayer is that you will be inspired, motivated, and encouraged to move forward in your walk with the Lord. None of us are perfect, nor will we achieve perfection in this life, but we can keep moving. Philippians 3:14–15 NKJV says, "I press toward the goal for the prize of the upward call of God in Christ Jesus. Therefore let us, as many as are mature, and have this mind; and if in anything you think otherwise, God will reveal even this to you."

FORTY-NINE

Ron and I have been married for forty-nine years at the time of the writing of this book. Our marriage has not been perfect. Marriage is certainly give and take. In the forty-nine years we've been married, we've learned a few things. It's not always about being right. It's about forgiving and also realizing it's not all about one person. What a shocker!

When we were in bible college, I wanted to be such a Suzy homemaker. One day, I decided to make homemade yeast bread to add to the amazing meal I had cooked. (I was 19 years old. I couldn't cook!) I had on my cute little apron and everything. I put the bread in the oven at 6:00 PM and we settled in to wait for the delicious bread to finish baking. We couldn't wait to slather on the butter and have it drip off our chins! I kept checking on it, looking at it, waiting for it to rise and get done. As I kept checking on it, it was getting browner and browner, but it wasn't rising and it didn't have that wonderful smell homemade bread is supposed to have.

At midnight, I took the dark brown little loaf of bread out of the oven and realized I had forgotten to put in the yeast. No wonder it wasn't smelling like bread! In a fit of rage I threw it on the kitchen floor, making a dent in the linoleum. Ron put his arm around me, told me it was okay and gave me a sweet kiss on the forehead as I stood there crying. I was crying because I had failed at making homemade bread and I was crying because I knew we might have to pay for the damaged floor.

On a different occasion during the same year of bible college, my husband wanted me to cook duck since he loves duck hunting. I put the duck in a pot and boiled it for what seemed to be an eternity. Finally, I put it on a plate and made my presentation. (Yes, I still had that same cute little apron on.) I was so proud of myself! He proceeded to slice the duck. I thought we were going to have to get a chainsaw, but he finally got it sliced. A big grin came across his face and I asked him what was wrong. No one told me I had to pick the feathers out of the meat with a toothpick, so it was full of feathers. Bon appetite, Baby!

In forty-nine years we have accumulated a lot of stories – true to life stories, funny stories, stories about difficulties in life and about the realness of God! We are still here, loving each other and loving God. I want to say to you young married couples, realize you aren't perfect, your partner's not perfect and your marriage won't be perfect. Just determine in the beginning to put God first, stay in church with a godly pastor, get involved in serving God and others, and always make it a point to spend quality time with each other. Learn early in your marriage to prioritize. You and your marriage will flourish and grow if you always put God first. One of these days you will wake up and you will have been married for forty-nine years. You will look up at each other with eyes of mercy and a heart full of love.

WAIT

But those that wait on the Lord shall renew their strength;
they shall mount up with wings like eagles, they shall run
and not be weary, they shall walk and not faint.
(Isaiah 40:31 NKJV)

The word wait means we have to be patient and not get in a hurry. For a person who's been overactive all their life, this is something hard to do. I usually want to run ahead, get there first, and be the first in line. I was always the kid with my hand up, waving at the teacher, wanting to be the first to answer the question. Of course I didn't know the answer, but I wanted to be the first. Patience has been a virtue I have had to work on all my life and I'm still working on it. I once had a minister tell me he envisioned me walking down a pathway with Jesus. Of course, I was walking way ahead and eventually he saw me turn and motion for Jesus to catch up.

Well, this is a pretty accurate description of me and the Lord for most of my adult life. This pretty much describes how I've reacted when the Lord shows me something. He will speak something to my heart or show me something and I have always thought NOW. I'm supposed to do that now. I would get so impatient when He didn't open the door or make a way. I would decide He needed my help so I would try to open my own doors, rushing ahead impatiently, then wondering why it all didn't work out. He does everything in His time, not ours. It took me such a long time to learn this lesson.

Wait means to stay or rest in patient expectation. It means to remain stationary until freedom of action has been given. Well, I don't like to wait. Is there anyone else out there like this or am I the only one? Let me just say, I've learned through the years to wait upon the Lord. I've learned to wait in expectation, expecting supernatural surprises. It's always better when we allow God to lead and we follow. Let me give you an example.

I had the same dream on three different occasions. I dreamt I was on stage leading praise and worship in Russia.

As I looked out over the audience, I saw Russians dressed in heavy coats and Ushanka hats. The people had their hands lifted and tears streamed down their faces as they worshiped the Lord. When I awoke I shared the dream with my husband, told him I was going to Russia, and I started praying and waiting for the opportunity to rise. I began to wonder if it was ever going to happen.

Fifteen years later, the opportunity arose for me to go with a group from our church to the Ukraine. I basically had forgotten about the three dreams until one night I was on stage playing and leading a group in worship. It wasn't until I looked out over the audience and saw the men and women in heavy coats and Ushanka hats with their hands lifted and tears streaming down their faces that I suddenly remembered. The Holy Spirit reminded me of the dreams.

What dream has the Lord placed in your heart? Have you waited and waited and still haven't seen any results? Just be patient and rest in expectation. Let Him lead and He will give you the desires of your heart. He will bring it to pass in His time if you put your trust in Him.

MEND

Do you have a friend in your life you were once close with? Did they hurt you or did you possibly hurt or offend them? Is it possible to salvage and save that friendship? If there is a chance, do you think you could forgive each other, reconcile, reconnect and be friends again? I'm not talking about reconnecting with toxic relationships or controlling friends. Think back… What was it that caused the rift between the two of you in the first place? Was it something childish and kind of silly now that you think about it?

We fight for those things that are important to us… a job promotion, our children, our loved ones. But what about that friendship where you had a disagreement over something so silly that you can't even remember what it was? Think of those relationships and ask yourself if they're worth reconciling. You may never be BFFs, but you might be able to at least be cordial to one another and be in the same room without feeling any animosity.

I've experienced forgiveness both ways where a close friend forgave me and where I've had to forgive someone who hurt me. Let's not allow jewels to slip through our hands because of pride, anger or competition. God is in the business of restoration. Look at those in the Bible who denied Him or talked about Him behind His back. He forgave.

I thank God for friendships restored. So much fun and so many good times we would have missed out on had we not forgiven each other and made the decision to move forward. Oh, the many laughs and good times that might have been lost if not for forgiveness. Think about it. Pray about it. If you feel a tug in your heart, make a coffee date and mend the bridges. Most of the time relationships can be resolved and restored with a great ending to the story. Who's the person that's coming to mind? I would think there are a lot of good times between the two of you that can still be had.

DIVINE INTERRUPTIONS

I saw God work today in such a special way. After bible study, I stopped by one of my favorite stores. Now y'all, I was on a shopping mission. As I walked in, I saw a friend who recently lost her son and I started visiting with her. I was just exhorting her and trying to be an encouragement to her in her time of need. I wasn't aware a sales clerk was listening to our conversation. After my friend left, I started looking at the sales rack and I made the statement, "Well, I don't know what I'm doing!" I was still a bit shaken by what my friend had been through and the time of ministry we just had in the middle of the store. The sales clerk, who had been working on the other side of the rack, looked up with tears in her eyes and said, "You are spreading the love of God!" Then the Lord opened the door for me to minister to her. Now, I didn't go shopping that day with the intention of ministering to people, but the needs were just there. The Holy Spirit divinely interrupted me!

I left there and went to a pharmacy to get a passport picture made. One of the employees at the photo center was extremely upset. She had misplaced her cell phone, thinking it had been stolen. She said, "I left it on the cart while I was stocking shelves." Three other employees were going all over the store looking for her phone. I walked over and asked the young lady, "Do you mind if we pray?" I took her hand and prayed this prayer... "Father God, if that phone is in this store, reveal it and show us where it is." It was just a quiet, simple prayer. I walked back over to the counter and almost immediately she yells, "Here it is! Here it is!" It was right by the cash register in plain open view. The other employees, all three of them said, "We looked there. We all searched all around that cash register. It wasn't there!" You can come up with your own explanation of how it got there in plain open view in an area they had all searched several times. As for me, I say it was divine intervention. I shared with them, "God cares about everything that concerns us." One of the other employees spoke up and said, "I like the way you said that. Did you all hear that? God cares about everything that concerns us! I like that!"

People are hungry and starving for something real to fill their hearts and lives. Jesus is the One and Only! Their lives were touched that day and God demonstrated His power to them. I only went in for a passport photo, but God! All of these divine connections happened in one day. God interrupted my plans and gave me opportunities to share His love and to be His hand extended. I encourage you today to be His hand extended. So many are oppressed. Let our prayer be that He would give us more divine connections, more opportunities and more divine interruptions!

CHILDLIKE

What a warm, sunny, beautiful fall day! I woke up this morning to His steadfast love and mercy, health, healing, a song in my heart, forgiveness, the gift of eternal life and the promise of spending eternity with Him! I woke up to peace, that kind of peace that passes all human understanding. Supernatural peace. When things are falling down around me, that Psalms 91 peace and assurance. I woke up in a nice warm bed, had an amazing cup of hot coffee – more cream than coffee – just the way I like it! I woke up with a roof over my head, a fridge full of food, and gas in my car. Did I mention the love of my family and friends? Just enjoying life and the blessings of the Lord. Can I encourage you to just stop, look, and listen? Stop looking at the negative things going on around you and around the world and focus on the beauty of God's creation.

When we were children, we didn't worry. Most of us grew up with parents who made sure we had a place to sleep, food to eat and everything we needed. A child usually doesn't worry because they know they will be protected and safe. We had childlike faith. We need to dig deep and once again find that inner child. We need to grab ahold of that childlike faith and trust our Heavenly Father to care for us. We need to trust that He is working all things together for good. Romans 8:28 says, "And we know that in all things God works for the good of those who love Him, who have been called according to His purpose." This Scripture doesn't mean we can live any way we choose and God will fix our messes. We can't quote the part of the scripture we like, "and we know that in all things God works for the good" and skip the rest, "of those who love Him, who have been called according to His purpose." God's telling us He can use all things together for good. He doesn't say all things are good.

Let's learn to put our childlike faith in Him and trust Him. Matthew 18:3 ESV says, "...Truly, I say to you, unless you turn and become like children, you will never enter the kingdom of heaven." Matthew 18:1–4 MSG says,

At about the same time, the disciples came

to Jesus asking, "Who gets the highest rank in God's kingdom?" For an answer Jesus called over a child, whom He stood in the middle of the room, and said, "I'm telling you, once and for all, that unless you return to square one and start over like children, you're not even going to get a look at the kingdom, let alone getting in. Whoever becomes simple and elemental again, like this child, will rank high in God's kingdom."

I encourage you to remember the innocence of a childlike behavior. A child loves without limits, doesn't focus on the faults of others and forgives easily. A child just enjoys playing and living a simple life. They love to play when the sun is shining and they love to play in the rain. How long has it been since you played in the rain? The next time it rains, walk outside, let the raindrops fall on your face and jump in the puddles. Become simple and elemental again. Become childlike.

A CHANCE

Have you ever been around a person that you are trying to have a conversation with and they seem to never take a breath? It's almost like you go to a happy place in your mind to just get relief from the constant talking. I've been thinking about that a lot lately and I can think of those that are that kind of conversationalist. I can also think of times I've been that way myself – dominating the conversation and our time together. The subject seems to be about me, myself and I. We want the other person to know our accomplishments, how much we are involved in, and how important we are. So, we boast and brag until we send the other person into his or her happy place in their mind (also known as tuning us out). It's when you're looking at the person, smiling and nodding your head but you aren't really there. I'm guilty.

Have you ever been talking to a friend or a family member and they never once asked how you are, how your family's doing, or ask about your life in any way? Or, have you been that person that is going on and on about your life, what you have accomplished, how all your family is and never once ask the other person about what's going on in their life? It is so annoying, isn't it? We need to practice the art of listening to what others are saying.

Let me approach this from a different angle. We need to practice the art of listening to what our heavenly Father is saying. When we go to the secret place with Him, do we dominate the conversation? Do we take time to enter His courts with thanksgiving and praise? Instead of starting with our long lists of what we want and what we need Him to do, do we even give Him a chance to speak?

Sometimes in His presence we confess, declare and make it known exactly what we want, need and are expecting from the Lord. Confessions and declarations are awesome and a very important part of our prayer life and conversation time with the Lord but sometimes we just need to be still in His presence and listen without interrupting Him when He's trying to speak to our hearts. Just breathe. Take a deep breath and give the Lord a chance to speak. He wants to tell us great and mighty things to come. He wants to lead, guide and direct us but He can't if we are the ones doing all the talking. He wants us to be still and just know that He is God.

God is so good. He loves. He listens. He rebukes. He chastises, leads, guides and directs. All He wants is for us to give Him a chance to speak and a chance to wrap His arms around us and let us know everything is going to be okay. Give place to the Spirit of God – inviting Him into your conversations. Just listen to His still, small voice and give Him a chance.

SURPRISES

Don't give up! Don't be discouraged! God has a plan – a divine plan for your life! The Bible tells us that God's ways are so much higher than our ways. We never want to question His ways – thinking our ways, our ideas or our plans are better. Did you know? Were you aware? He has a surprise plan for our lives! It's so exciting! Don't you just love surprises? I know I do! The Lord is the best gift giver ever. He knows what we like and He knows what we need. Scripture tells us that He knows what we have need of even before we ask. Can you imagine that?

On more than one occasion He has given me peace that surpasses all understanding. Joy unspeakable. You know, the kind of joy that is just unexplainable. He has given me sweet sleep, free from stress and worry. I think one of my favorite gifts He's given me is to be my ever-present help in my time of need. Did I mention forgiveness? Not just being forgiven, but to be able to forgive those who have hurt me.

He has given me gifts of healing and deliverance, the smiles of my family and grandchildren and the gift of friends. Oh, how I treasure those gifts! Oh my goodness, the gift of laughter! When I can't seem to find my way, He's there to light my path.

Take a few moments and think about all the special gifts God has given you. Think about all the surprises He has brought your way and blessed you with. A surprise is something unexpected or astonishing that may be eye opening or causes someone to be in shock. God has Holy Ghost inspired surprises! All those prayers we've been standing in faith, believing Him to answer... He's going to answer them when we least expect it and we will be astonished by the way He chooses to answer. Let's open our eyes, wait for, expect, and anticipate those Holy Ghost surprises and answers to our prayers. We will wake up one morning, expecting to say the same prayers over the same things, and the Spirit of God will say, "Surprise!"

FORGIVE

It was December 23rd and I was preparing for Christmas, doing the usual things – wrapping gifts, drinking hot chocolate and thinking of what I was going to serve for our annual Christmas family brunch. I think we even had a roaring fire in the fireplace.

Finally, around 9 o'clock that evening, I was able to sit down and rest. I was making a list of all the things I still had left to do, when the phone rang. It was one of those calls you don't ever want to receive. The voice at the other end said, "Mrs. Carroll, this is the Shreveport police and I'm calling you to inform you your son has been hurt and is in route to the hospital." In an instant, everything changed. In place of the emotions of happiness, joy, peace and contentment, I felt fear, anger, dread and I think I even felt a little rage. I experienced emotions I didn't even know I had. How could this be happening to our family? Why is this happening to this family? God what did we do wrong to deserve this? A few weeks later, I realized that bad things happen to good people. It's called life! The difference is that as Christians, we have the Lord to hold our hand and walk us through the challenges of life.

The police told us when we arrived that my son had been attacked and stabbed multiple times. The person who did it was someone he knew and who had been in our home on many occasions. I know this is heavy for a devotional, but this is a testimony of the power of forgiveness... a choice we have to make to be able to move forward in life to set ourselves free and to set the person who wronged us free. We can only do that with the help of Jesus Christ.

One afternoon, about three weeks after the incident, I was sitting in my big comfy chair where I meet with the Lord and have sweet conversations with Him. You know, that special place, that secret place. I was praying and reading the Word. In my conversation with the Lord I said, "Lord, I choose to forgive this person for trying to kill my son. I forgive them." Immediately, I felt the sense of being really spiritual – super spiritual. In the next breath I said, "I forgive them, but this person will never set foot in my house again. Never!"

As I sat there, feeling really holy and super spiritual, the Holy Spirit spoke to my heart. I heard the quiet voice of His Spirit say, "When you have hurt Me or grieved My Spirit, have I ever said you could never set foot in My house?" "But God, this is a person who hurt my son! I have a right!"

I realized right then and there, I had not truly forgiven this person. I went through the motions I thought necessary, but the Holy Spirit, being the comforter He is, knew I had not truly forgiven. He knew I could not continue on in my life, experiencing the joy of the Lord, if I could not totally let it go. In time, I was able to totally forgive and let go of all the negative emotions. Our whole family was able to move on in our lives because of the grace of God.

The person, of course, is no longer part of our lives but the reason the Holy Spirit spoke to me was to help me lead our whole family into total and complete forgiveness so we could move forward. No more unforgiveness. No more bondage to negative emotions. He also spoke to my heart that my attitude would be the catalyst in how our family would heal from this. The choices I made and how I handled this would affect my whole family and how they handled it. A catalyst is someone or something that causes significant change or action. In other words, the Holy Spirit was saying my attitude could bring about change in my family. I choose forgiveness. Real forgiveness. We've had several Christmas holidays since that time and they have been wonderful and peaceful.

The Word of God tells us it is Satan who comes to steal, kill and destroy our lives. Has he attacked you, your family or friends? Has he tried to bring devastation in your family? Have you asked, "Why us? What do we do to deserve this?" If you are still holding a grudge, anger, frustration or unforgiveness in your heart, turn those emotions over to the Lord and ask Him to help you let go. He's forgiven us of all our sins and all we have done that has displeased Him. He loves us and gives us an open invitation to come to His house anytime – regardless of what we have done.

God was not requiring us to literally open the doors of our home and invite this person for pizza but He was requiring us, as a family, to totally forgive. He was requiring more than a superficial attitude of forgiveness, but genuine forgiveness, so that we could be free and live a happy, joyful, blessed and abundant life.

RETURNING

This morning, as I was having my first cup of coffee for the day, I was reminded of a bedtime story my dad used to tell me about a little boy who ran away from home at 15 years old. That little boy, of course, being him. My dad was raised by his grandfather in a small town in Texas. They didn't have a lot and his granddad was a farmer. They lived a simple life.

When my dad was 15 years old, he decided to get out and see what there was to life outside of this small little farming community. So, without letting his granddad know, he hopped on a train and left. He was gone for a year, going from city to city searching to fill a void in his heart, not knowing that only Jesus could satisfy his soul. One day, a year later, he decided he wanted to go home. So, he headed home not knowing if Granddad would be mad or if he would even let him in. When he got off the train, he started walking home. Granddad was working in the fields, planting. Dad said he was so scared and nervous not knowing what kind of reception he was going to get. He said Granddad's back was to him and all of a sudden, as if Granddad sensed he was there, he stood up and slowly turned around. Dad said he threw the garden hoe up in the air and with open arms came running. With tears streaming down his face he said, "Son, why didn't you let me know you were leaving? I would have given you some money. So glad to see you!" Granddad wasn't angry with him, didn't scold or rebuke him, but just welcomed him with open arms.

This reminds me of the parable in the Bible of the prodigal son (see Luke 15:11–32). The Father invites us to return home. He is waiting with open arms to receive us. He's not going to point out what we've done wrong or scold us about our wrong choices. He just wants us home in His Kingdom – the Kingdom of God. He has a table spread, anticipating the return of His children. Such a beautiful homecoming He has planned. I encourage you today, regardless of where your travels have taken you, no matter how far you've strayed away, just come home!

CHEERFUL

I can be serious when I want to. But who wants to? Proverbs 17:22 NKJV says, "A merry heart does good, like medicine, but a broken spirit dries the bones." The MSG puts it this way, "A cheerful disposition is good for your health; gloom and doom leave you bone-tired!" There is enough doom, gloom, despair, and depression in the world. I say let's spread a little cheer, a little joy of the Lord. When we enter a room and have fellowship with others, we should leave them feeling better than before they saw us.

I remember when my husband had an accident in early 2000. He fell nine feet from a roof and broke several bones. In the emergency room, the doctor told us he may need surgery, there was a possibility he wouldn't walk out of the hospital and we could expect about an eight-week hospital stay. Of course we had people everywhere praying and believing God with us for a miracle. The doctor came in the next day and told us he wasn't going to do surgery because he felt the bones would mend on their own. God was already working.

One day during our hospital stay we were feeling pretty down. The pain, the depression, and being unsure if my husband would be able to work again began to get to us. You know, that *why did this happen to us* syndrome. We were living right, serving God, and going to church. Why did this have to happen? We had never had anything like this happen in our family. My husband never had a headache in his life. It was unnerving to see him lying there in pain and unable to move. To be honest, I was dealing with fear.

One day I bought a *Reader's Digest* and brought it to the hospital room. I turned to the page where all the jokes and funny stories were. I began to read joke after joke. In a few moments we were just laughing until tears streamed down our cheeks. Part of the tears was pent up emotions and part was just laughter. To be honest, some of the jokes weren't funny at all, actually kind of corny, but there was a release that came with the laughter and a healing that came as well.

The joy of the Lord began to strengthen us.

The Lord brought healing that day. Day by day, things improved. The eight-week hospital stay ended up only being ten days. No surgery was needed and my husband began to make progress from that day forward. We literally laughed our way out of depression!

Whatever your situation is today, whatever you are facing, make a choice to be cheerful and to allow the joy of the Lord to strengthen and heal you. A cheerful, merry heart is the best medicine and will bring healing to your mind, your body, and your emotions.

AFFIRMATION

An affirmation is a word of encouragement, emotional support or an endorsement. I don't know of anyone who doesn't like or enjoy being appreciated. I know scripture tells us to encourage ourselves in the Lord just like King David did. I know we are to live by faith and not by sight. I know we are to declare and speak the Word of God over ourselves and our challenges in life. But once in a while, it's nice to hear words of affirmation, encouragement and appreciation from others. Everyone occasionally wants to hear... Great job! You are really good at that! Just keep trying, you'll get it! I really appreciate all you do! You are such a blessing!

I've come to realize the person who is always faithful, always dependable and does a great job, may not always be there. We should not take for granted they will be, but be thankful and express our gratitude to them. If I am your friend or family member and I see you are not yourself, there's probably a good reason for that. If I see you struggling or you seem a little down, I need to be a friend who encourages you.

I want to be that kind of friend, family member, employee or employer, minister or staff person who cares. I want to offer you a helping hand and let you know there's hope in your situation. I want to speak words over you that will lift up and encourage your heart. "Can I take you to lunch?" "Do you want to go for coffee?" Sometimes when we discern someone is struggling, we don't have to get into a deep conversation about what's going on, but we can give a compliment. "You look really nice today. Did you get a new outfit?" "I want you to know what a great friend you are. I appreciate our friendship." These are simple words of affirmation.

We never know when the person we're with has had abusive words spoken to them as they go out the door. Let's be a ray of sunshine and speak affirmative words over them and to them. We are to be a light in the darkness. If we want to be appreciated, let's appreciate others!

IMPORTANT

Insignificant means irrelevant, unimportant, meaningless, pointless and too small to be worth consideration. The Lord wants us to know, we are significant, we are important and our lives have meaning. We have hope and a future (see Jeremiah 29:11). He wants us to know He considers us. He knows everything about us because He created us in His image. We are worth more than all the riches of this world. In spite of what you've been told or made to believe by harmful words spoken to you, your life has meaning. Jesus gave His all for us and He wants us to have an abundant, prosperous, joyful, Spirit-filled life! Nothing less.

We were traveling one day and stopped at a restaurant for breakfast. It was really busy this particular morning so they had four cooks. One focused only on making pancakes and waffles. One made all the eggs. There was another guy who made all the toast and the fourth cooked all the bacon. This guy fried so much bacon and every piece he cooked was perfect. Not a single piece was overcooked or undercooked. I watched him for a little while then I motioned him to come to our table. I asked him, "How do you cook that bacon so perfect?" I was totally serious because I either undercook or overcook it all the time! Suddenly, the biggest smile came across his face. I had made him feel important about his job. I'm sure that possibly he wasn't used to getting compliments on his bacon frying skills! I asked him for some tips (the Lord knew I needed them). As we were leaving, I overheard him giving someone else a compliment. We complemented him, he complemented someone else, and I'm sure it went from one person to another for the rest of the day.

If you spread sincere heartfelt compliments and make others feel significant, it creates a chain reaction. Maybe you are dissatisfied with where you are in life right now. Just be the best you can be right now wherever you are. You are important. God considers you and your life is significant. God has a purpose, a plan and a destiny for you!

PSA 6:1

A few years ago Ron, my husband, was diagnosed with prostate cancer. I received a letter from the doctor's office and handwritten on the letter with a black sharpie pen was *PSA 6:1*. I thought it was so nice of the office to send a scripture to encourage us and that there must be a few Christians working there. So, I proceeded to look up Psalms 6:1. It read, "Lord, do not rebuke me in your anger or discipline me in your wrath." I thought, "Well, what in the world does this have to do with anything?"

It was kind of them to try to encourage us, so, I called the office to thank them for the "encouraging" scripture. The nurse said, "Hun, what Scripture?" I said, "You know. The one you wrote at the top of the page with a black sharpie pen... PSA 6:1." After all the office had stopped howling with laughter, the nurse said (in between snorts of laughter), "Mrs. Carroll, that wasn't a scripture. That was your husband's PSA level." So, in the midst of adversity and a bad report, we all had a good laugh! Of course the joke was on me! That was 10 years ago and still to this day every time we go in that office we all have a good laugh!

You know, when the joy of the Lord is our strength, we can face bad news or a bad report and somewhere in the midst of it all we can find joy to face another day. The scripture is true... a merry heart does do good like a medicine because a glad and joyful heart helps in healing. Proverbs 17:22 says, "A cheerful heart is good medicine, but a crushed spirit dries up the bones."

Ron has been cancer free for over 10 years now. He is cheerful, his heart is full of joy, and he's glad to be alive and doing well. We are so thankful the Lord wasn't rebuking us in anger and He wasn't pouring His wrath out on us. He was merely making our hearts merry and glad. He was giving us a good laugh as He was healing Ron's body!

CALL

For "whoever calls on the name
of the Lord shall be saved."
(Romans 10:13 NKJV)

Several years ago my son was working in Minden, Louisiana for a railroad company. One afternoon he was visiting us and I felt the Holy Spirit prompting me to tell him, "Son, if you ever get into a situation that's threatening, just call on the name of Jesus." I quoted Romans 10:13 and left it at that. Two weeks later, he was on the job late at night in the dimly lit area. He walked out to check the grounds. As he was walking back to the office, a man jumped out of the shadows, sprayed him with mace, put a gun to his head, and demanded his wallet and money.

In the early hours of the morning, our son rang our doorbell. His face was red and blistered and his eyes were watering. He was obviously shaken and in shock. As he shared with us what had happened, I asked him, "Son, what did you do?" He said, "Mom, I remembered the scripture you shared with me about calling on Jesus if I ever got into a dangerous or threatening position. I fell to my knees and screamed *Jesus* as loud as I could. When I did, the man grabbed my wallet and ran."

A few days later the man was caught. He not only had attacked my son, but he had attacked and shot a man days earlier who was taking his trash out, robbing him of five dollars. Whoever calls on the name of the Lord shall be saved! Saved means to protect, rescue and keep someone's life safe. That's what Jesus did for my son. He protected, rescued and saved his life!

Whatever you face, call on Jesus. He will save, protect and rescue you. There is no other name than the name of Jesus Christ. There are so many scriptures that instruct us to call on Him in the time of trouble. Psalms 50:15 says, "Call on Me in the day of trouble; I will deliver you, and you will honor Me."

Psalms 116:2 NKJV says, "Because He has inclined His

ear to me, therefore I will call upon Him as long as I live." As for me and my house, we have learned to do just that. We call upon Him, honor Him, and we will continue to do so all the days of our lives.

BLESSED

"By the help of God, I am through with whiskey.
You have broke me from drinking. I love you and
may God be with us."

This is a note written by my father, Pastor W. T. Keeling, written sometime in the late 40s. My mom and dad were newlyweds, but my father had a severe problem with drinking. They lived in a small apartment and had only one car. My dad was out late one night, drinking as usual. My mom had been asleep when she was awakened by a dream. She dreamt my dad was sitting on a railroad track, the car had stalled and he was passed out slumped over the steering wheel. She immediately got up, went to the neighbor's house and asked to borrow their car. She left and drove to the only railroad track in the small little town. Just like in her dream, there was their car, stalled on the track with my dad passed out and a train coming full speed. She immediately got in the car and drove it off the track. She saved my dad's life thanks to the dream the Lord gave her, warning her of the danger he was in. Thank you Lord for the Holy Ghost!

It was after this episode that he wrote this note to her, and God was with them. He never drank again! They began attending Life Tabernacle in Shreveport, Louisiana under the leadership of Pastor Jack and Mildred Moore. There, they gave their hearts to the Lord and began serving God together. My dad's testimony of being delivered from alcohol is in one of the archived *Christ for the Nations Magazine* and in a 1952 issue of *The Shreveport Times*. Jesus Christ saved my dad's life, filled him with the Holy Spirit and together my parents pastored churches for many, many years. They also traveled and did missionary evangelist work all through Mexico – preaching, holding revivals, leading people to salvation all over the country of Mexico until he was in his seventies.

At the end of his life, he was diagnosed with dementia. One day, he had been in the intensive care unit recovering from a stroke. The doctors told us when he woke up he might use foul language, be a little combative, and might need to be restrained. He was trying to prepare us. When my dad finally awoke, I was sitting by his bedside. He looked over at me and said, "Honey, you should have been with me. I just came back from Mexico and over 250 people got saved and filled with the Holy Ghost. I didn't even have to lay hands on them. I just told them to lay hands on their neighbor, I led them in the prayer of salvation, then instructed them on how to receive the Holy Ghost! It was the best revival I've ever held!"

You see, in his mind, he had been in Mexico leading a revival, getting people saved and filled with the Holy Spirit – not in an ICU hospital room. No cursing, no violence, just leading people to Jesus! This is the same man who at one time had a drinking problem until he turned his life over to the Lord. The Lord changed his heart, gave him a new life, and led him in a new direction – bringing his life from broken to blessed. Jesus wants to do the same for you!

KALEIDOSCOPE

I wonder how many friends we have lost over the years because we've looked at someone and prejudged them without knowing anything about them and without knowing what they've been through to get to where they are now. We often choose to form an opinion without giving people a chance. Maybe we shut them out or not included them in our social circle. We've already decided they aren't the kind of person we want to socialize with. Our decision is based on an assumption, a belief, a guess or a speculation. It is possible we have let a diamond slip through our fingers. We've made an assumption based on her outfit, her style, or some other shallow guess about who she is. I would venture to say we have all done this at some time or another.

A kaleidoscope is a toy that you can look through the end and it has a constantly changing pattern of beautiful colors. If you ever look through the eye of this toy and turn it, the loose bits of colored glass move and are reflected off mirrors, giving you delightful results that are so diverse and fun. When making friends and meeting new people, be open to a diverse collection. When we choose friends wisely, they may look different or have opposite personalities to ours. They may have different backgrounds, talents and giftings. We will always have friends that enhance us and we will enhance them. Let's just be careful we don't let those beautiful shards of glass slip through our hands that could form diverse patterns in our lives. They can be delightful and fun, adding diversity to our kaleidoscope of friends!

STEP UP

Settle down your spirit through the Word of God. I speak peace to you today. He is in love with you! He is watching over you to fulfill His Word and plan in your life. Whatever the future holds for you, God will carry out His purposes in your life. Listen, His power is at your disposal. His presence hovers around you. What are you afraid of? He tells us to fear not because He is with us. This is a year of change in your life. Don't be afraid to let Him work, rearrange and change your future. Don't be afraid of what people will say. Don't be afraid of your lack of ability. If He has called you, He will equip you.

Don't fear, don't dread, don't be shy or apprehensive. Allow a holy boldness to partner with you and assist you. Be bold and be strong for the Lord thy God is with you.

"...Be strong and courageous. Do not be afraid; do not be discouraged, for the Lord your God will be with you wherever you go." (Joshua 1:9).

It's okay to have dreams that far exceed what you think you're capable of. Put fear under your feet and extend your hand. Grab for what He has for you in confidence that He will perform His work in you and through you. Step up and step out! Flourish in your God-given gifts.

COMPLIMENTS

I absolutely love when ladies compliment, encourage, promote and lift each other up. The enemy wants us to gossip, compete, and be jealous of one another. He wants us to try to feel superior over another, to compete for attention or pats on the back, or to feel like we have to be number one. It's so much more fun and fulfilling to build our sisters up, to brag about their accomplishments and successes, and to talk about what concerns them. It feels good to allow them to be first once in a while and to step back and let them to be in the limelight.

Let's not be insecure and concerned someone is going to get ahead of us. We need to spiritually grow up! It's okay if someone gets in line ahead of us. It's okay if someone excels. Compliment them. Promote them. Support them.

It's such a joy seeing people promote each other and help each other fulfill their dreams. It's true. If you help others fulfill their dreams, God will send someone along to help you fulfill yours. That's just God's way!

If we want friends, we need to be a friend. We have to love our friends the same way we want to be loved. If we'll do this, God will see to it that we have lots of wonderful friends who actually care about what goes on with us. If we are jealous, competitive, gossipers, and run others down to build ourselves up, we'll be able to count our friends on one hand. I want my cup running over and spilling out with good friends and relationships. So let's choose to respect, value, honor, love, and promote each other. That's the lifestyle of a Christian.

THE RING

Okay, explain this. One Wednesday night at church I lost a ring. I had taken it off to put on hand lotion (of all things) and left it in my lap, forgetting about it. I guess it fell on the floor when we stood up to be dismissed. We were sitting close to the front in the middle section. I'm just assuming that's what happened because when I got home I noticed it wasn't on my finger. I looked everywhere, searching my purse and could not find it.

Four days later, on Sunday morning, we were sitting toward the back of the church on the left side of the sanctuary. It's important you understand where we were sitting both times. We sat in a totally different place than we usually sit and it was for a reason. As a matter of fact, we have never sat in this area of the church, but for some reason we did this particular morning. As I sat down after praise and worship, I looked at the floor. There by my foot was my ring – shining and sparkling. I stared at it in disbelief. (You know sometimes God blesses us with a supernatural blessing and we don't know how to respond!)

So, I'm trying to logically figure out how a ring got from where I sat at the front of the church four days ago to the back of the church right by my foot. It wasn't under the seat. It wasn't under the chair in front of where I was sitting. It was right by my left foot so I would see it shining up at me. I choose to believe it was a miracle. There's no other way in my mind to explain it. Be ready for your miracle! However God has to do it, He will give us miracles. Let's not stand there, staring our miracle in the face, wondering how it happened. Let's just believe it and receive it!

BOWING

And here I am your invited guest – it's incredible! I enter
your house; here I am, prostrate in your inner sanctum,
waiting for directions to get me safely through enemy lines.
(Psalms 5:7–8 MSG)

Bowing is an act of worship. It means to yield, submit, recognize, and to acknowledge. It is the highest form of worship. We are to enter His gates with thanksgiving and His courts with praise. We sing, we dance, we shout, we lift up holy hands, but often we stop there and never bow. We fail to submit, yield, recognize or honor Him by bowing in reverence. If we bow to someone, we agree to do what they want. If we want to get safely through enemy lines, then let's bow before the King of Kings and Lord of lords – reverencing Him, honoring Him and agreeing to let Him do what He wants in every situation.

I grew up with an altar in our church where we bowed and prayed at the end of service – kneeling in reverence before Him and submission to Him. Those were some awesome times around the altar, bowing in His presence.

When I was 18 years old and about to leave for college, I got up one evening around 2 AM to get a drink of water and saw my dad in his office, on his knees. He was praying for me, crying out to God. I heard him say, "Lord, use her for your glory." I have never forgotten seeing my dad on his knees, tears streaming down his face, praying and asking God to use me for His glory.

There's just something about kneeling and bowing. I have difficulty finding the right words to describe it. Sometimes when the glory of God is so strong and His presence so heavy, I can't hardly stand. It's in those times I know I am standing in the presence of a holy God, on holy ground, and I bow!

MOVE

Do you want to get out of that rut you've been in? Then take decisive steps to move forward. If you are in a rut, you are stuck, your wheels are spinning and you're going nowhere. It's time to get out of that place and move forward! You may stride, strut, prance or tiptoe, but just move! You've been in this pit long enough. It's time to bust a move and go forward. Whatever method you choose to move, do it with all your strength.

Declare the word of God and what He says about the circumstance you're facing. Praise and worship your way out. Gideon marched around the walls of Jericho, singing praises for seven days until the walls fell. I know you're tired of feeling bummed out and just crummy. It's time to put on your spiritual dancing shoes and dance your way out! Jesus died on the cross for you to have an abundant life. A life filled with joy peace and contentment. Yet sometimes we're sitting in the ditch, just spinning our wheels and going nowhere. Let's move forward!

Look, there are several ways to move forward and walk out of the rut. If you choose to strut, stride, prance, or tiptoe, just choose a method and move! To stride is to take long decisive steps. To strut is to parade and showoff. Show the enemy you're coming out of this! Strut your stuff and come out of that ditch of despair and depression. To prance is to walk in an animated manner while waving your arms. This one is my favorite! Come out of that despair in an animated manner, waving your arms. Wave your arms in the face of the enemy, strutting your stuff, taking long strides until you're completely free. Just move! Go forward!

JEWELS

Friends are absolute jewels. A beautiful treasure God has gifted us with. He sends different people across our path for us to be a blessing and vice versa. Here's a description of some of my jewel friends.

Some of my friends are rubies. They are loyal and inspire emotion. They inspire my emotions to be up when they are down. A ruby is considered the most magnificent of all gems, the queen of stones and the stone of kings. It surpasses all other precious stones in virtue and it is considered a stone of nobility. Its value exceeds even that of the diamond. Listen to this, my ruby friends. A ruby symbolizes the sun and its glowing color symbolizes an inextinguishable flame.

Some of you are sapphires! You are stone of wisdom,

speaking words of wisdom into my life. A sapphire is a transparent, precious stone. My sapphire friends are transparent, genuine and real.

Some of my friends are a beautiful topaz. You produce fire! You are a symbol of hope and you set a fire under me that produces hope when I feel hopeless. You always inspire me to move forward.

Some of you are emeralds. You bring freshness and vitality to my spirit. Emerald means love unconditionally. An emerald brings freshness and vitality into a friendship. It is a stone of inspiration and patience.

Some of you are diamonds. You symbolize faithfulness, love and purity. No matter what, you are there.

And to the pearls in my life, you are of great rarity and worth. You, my pearl friends, are highly prized. You are pearls of wisdom, speaking wisdom into my life and spirit.

Whatever category you fall into, you are priceless, valuable, faithful, inspiring, loyal, loving and kind! Treasures that can never be replaced. When we get to the end of life, the most valuable treasures we can have are our friends.

PRESS ON

Today I started back walking after getting off my routine schedule. We've been remodeling and I just couldn't seem to make the time. (I really could have because most of us make time for what we really want to do!) Usually when I walk I combine lunges, power walking, arm exercises, and jumping jacks. I will also set a goal and tell myself things like, "Okay, power walk to that stop sign."

Today, I was tempted to stop and turn around just a few steps from my goal. My muscles were screaming at me and I was so tired. After all, it had been a while since I had last exercised. I thought, "Well, it won't matter. I'm just a few feet away. It won't make a big difference." It probably wouldn't have made a difference as far as burning calories or strengthening my muscles but it would make a difference in the fact that I didn't want to press on and finish my commitment. I wanted to stop short of my goal. That made a big difference! Then, I made a decision. I decided to keep walking in spite of the pain and discomfort. I continued and power walked all the way to my goal. As a matter fact, I started running, just to get there faster. Was it hard? Yes! Did it hurt? Yes! Was it painful? Yes! But I made it. And guess what... you can too!

Sometimes we're tempted to just stop a few feet from our goal, our destiny. The enemy whispers, "Why don't you just stop, give up, turn around. It won't matter. It's no big deal." When something's painful, uncomfortable, or hurts, we often times want to stop before we reach our breakthrough. Look, it's not how long it takes us to get there, it's about finishing and completing what is set before us. We can do it when our goal is in view. Just start running towards it. Just finish. Press on!

MASTER BUILDER

My husband built a beautiful home on the lake for us where we raised our two boys. There, as a family, we made some beautiful memories with friends and family. There was lots of fishing with the boys, barbecues and fish fries. We lived there for six years and for most of those six years we struggled. It was during the recession of the 80s.

One of the miracles of those years is a testimony of God's delivering power. We, like many other people, were struggling financially. During this time, we pastored Harvest Time Church. My husband closed our remodeling business for a year to build a beautiful new church facility, so, we lived on our savings.

After the church was completed, we reopened our business, put the ad back in the newspaper, and waited for the calls to pour in. We thought the next week we would start getting business calls. After all, we had sacrificed and lived on our savings as we donated our time and labor to the new building. Finally, after standing on the Word of God that He would supply all our needs according to His riches in glory, we received a phone call and secured a job that was more than all the savings we had spent while we worked on the church! God is faithful! Eventually, we sold that house and built another one about two miles away. We left memories of miracles behind and looked forward to the new memories we would make.

One afternoon, about two months ago, our old home caught on fire. It was totally destroyed. There was nothing left but the foundation. I walked up to see what used to be our home where we raised our boys. I stood in what was once our kitchen and dining room. Memories flooded my mind. All of a sudden, it dawned on me... the foundation is still intact. It wasn't damaged by the flames or devastation. It's ready to be built upon again. Someone was going to buy that lot and rebuild a beautiful, new, modern home on that foundation and it will be stronger and better than ever.

There are times in life when it seems we have been knocked totally off our foundation – devastated by the fires of the enemy, by the storms, the wind and the rain. But it's not the end of the road. I know the Master Builder. His name is Jesus! He will take the devastation life has sent our way and rebuild on that foundation, making all things new again! Second Corinthians 5:17 NKJV says, "Therefore, if anyone is in Christ, he is a new creation; old things have passed away; behold, all things have become new." If your foundation is built on Christ, the Solid Rock, He can rebuild your life. Ask Him. He will take what looks like devastation, turn it around, and make something beautiful out of your life! He is the Master Builder.

ANOINTING

Once you know Jesus, you will never ever be the same. He paid it all on Calvary for our freedom – to be free from sin and to live an abundant life. So, why do we see so much talent and ability but a lack of anointing? It's the anointing that makes the difference. Without it, it's just a person with a talent.

I want to see and feel the kind of anointing when someone ministers or sings that absolutely pierces my heart and soul. The kind of anointing that brings me to my knees, stirs a spirit of reverence, and causes me to bow in His presence. That kind of anointing that makes me want to shout, sing, laugh and dance.

Lord, I ask You to fill me with power from on high. I'm not singing one word or playing one note on an instrument without your anointing. Sing through me, play through me, speak through me. I choose to lay aside the technology of today to draw close to You, to be filled with Your Spirit. I want to linger and stay awhile in Your presence until I feel I've touched You, until I break through into a freedom in Your presence.

When we linger we stay longer than necessary and are reluctant to leave because we're enjoying where we are. Yes, Lord! I want to draw near to You, linger, and stay awhile in Your presence until I feel I've touched You. Until I know beyond a shadow of a doubt, I've been in Your presence, sitting at Your feet.

Psalms 42:1 NKJV says, "As the deer pants for the water brooks, so pants my soul for You, O God." I am craving, seeking, panting, and lingering in His presence. I'm longing for His anointing to rest upon me and flow out of me. If He's not Lord of all, He's not Lord at all!

RENOVATIONS

We're doing some much-needed renovations to our 30 year old home. The hardest thing so far has been to replace the hardwood floors. They're covered with water stains, scratches, and a big discolored circle where our dining table sat and the sun bleached the floors around it.

This floor has really been resistant to the changes. It's not coming up in large pieces, but more like splinters. It's really stuck to the concrete. To be honest, it's been a nightmare! The new floors cannot go over the old floors. All the old wood has to come up. The concrete has to be cleaned, made smooth, and all the debris from the old floors removed. It's holding up progress because it has been so resistant to change!

Sometimes we are like these old hardwood floors –

resisting the changes the Holy Spirit wants to bring into our lives and our ministries. We need to allow the Spirit of God to come in, clean out our debris, and make our old surfaces clean and smooth so He can install the new. Let's not resist progress.

Can we just look past the mess right now and envision how beautiful the completed project will be? If we can do that, it will help us get past what we see right now. Let's get a picture of how beautiful and clean our lives will be when God gets through with the renovations. When all the dust clears, the old thrown out and the new put in, how much better our lives will be. Let's make a decision today and ask the Lord to come in and do all the renovations He needs to do in our heart, our soul and our mind. Change us Lord. Renovate and renew us!

SECRET PLACE

Come to me, all you who are weary and
burdened, and I will give you rest.
(Matthew 11:28)

There is a special place, a secret place in God's presence, where you can take a break and unwind. Just lean back in His arms and let Him carry you through the storm. He will bring you to a place found only in His presence that will give you relief from the high winds and the crashing waves of life.

Sometimes we get so wound up from the stress and challenges of life that we just need to take a deep breath. Rest means to be placed, supported, and to stay in a specified position. Don't let the enemy displace you from your position. Stay! Don't allow distractions. Take authority over distractions and interruptions.

Rest is a weapon given to us by God. The enemy hates it because he wants us to burn out, be preoccupied, and our time filled with good things and busyness. We need to focus on God commitments – things He wants us to do and be involved in. If we are so busy that we never enter into that secret place or have special time with Him, we will find ourselves weary in doing well. Jesus says in Matthew that His yoke is easy and His burden is light. He wants us free to worship, free to enjoy life, busy doing God-things and not just good things everyone else wants us to do.

Get in His presence and find out what He wants you to be committed to. Find rest, relaxation and relief in His presence. In His presence there is fullness of joy. Not in the works we do for Him, but in His presence is where we can live in an attitude of peace. The only one we have to please in this life is Jesus and He is the only one who can satisfy us.

Come with Me by yourselves to a quiet place
and get some rest. (Mark 6:31b)

The Lord replied, "My Presence will go with you, and I
will give you rest." (Exodus 33:14)

Be still before the Lord and wait patiently for Him.
(Psalm 37:7a)

Take some time in this busy world to rest and refresh. He's waiting for you in the secret place!

TRUTH

Have fun! No holier than thou attitude. Superficial. Just taking on the personality of whomever you're with at the time. Stay away from sin, avoid temptation and learn to enjoy the simple things in life. If you fall, get up and move on! Don't just lie there on the ground feeling sorry for yourself and making no effort to get up. You may be cast down or knocked down, but you are not destroyed. I promise, it's not the end of the world!

Laugh, smile, love others and love yourself. You are the righteousness of God in Christ Jesus. We are imperfect people who live in an imperfect world. But God! Make people laugh and learn to laugh at yourself. Make people smile and smile at yourself. Don't judge. Remember, how you dish it out is how it's coming back at you!

Let God be God. All the things you tend to worry about and stress over, just learn to let God handle it! It's so much easier. Live in an attitude of peace and maintain a spirit of joy. That situation you've been so worried about, just let God work it out. One morning you will wake up and it will be turned around. I know! I've had it happen to me!

Don't pause or put your life on hold because of adversity. He wants us to continue with an abundantly happy and joy-filled life. Go ahead! Enjoy your day! Leap for joy, laugh, shout, dance before the Lord. Drink in His presence. This is the day the Lord has made. Go ahead... Have a blessed day!

HAVE A HEART

Sometimes we don't like to talk about pain because we're afraid of being judged as weak, not having faith, or being negative. We lack empathy for each other. What is empathy? It is the ability to understand and share the feelings of another person. Sometimes people are flippant, showing no mercy or empathy. I didn't say sympathy, or feeling sorry for someone. I'm saying we often times lack the ability to show mercy or put ourselves in another person's position and trying to understand how they feel. That's being empathetic.

To be empathetic is to be sensitive to the needs of others. It's being understanding and putting yourself in another person's position instead of criticizing them for how they're handling the situation in their life. Another way of saying it is simply to have a heart! Isaiah 53:4 tells us how Jesus was and is touched by the feelings of our infirmities. If we are sick in body, sick in mind or emotions, or heartsick, He is touched by our feelings. He desires for us to reach out and touch Him so He can heal our pain.

The pain of divorce is real. The pain of a prodigal son or daughter is real. The pain of rejection or feeling left out is real. The pain of losing a friend or loved one to death is real. The pain of chronic fatigue and sickness is real. The pain of a bad health report is real. There is nothing weak or faithless in admitting we are in pain in any of these areas of our lives. The weakness or lack of faith comes when we don't stand and fight against what is trying to destroy us. Pain brings discouragement, depression, despair and the feeling of hopelessness. We cannot give up and give in and not fight. Face the truth. Face the circumstance. Fight the good fight of faith. Put on the whole armor of God. Surely He has borne all our grief and sorrows and by His stripes we are healed!

We can be restored, renewed, revived, refreshed. We are blessed with the opportunity of choices and new beginnings. It is a new day! Don't face another day, carrying the pain of life's challenges. Get to know the

Peace Speaker and know Him by name. Jesus! He is the giver of life. It's okay to say, "Lord, my heart is broken. I'm a basket case. I'm hurting. Lord, I know You have experienced grief and pain and suffering. I know You understand how I feel. That's why I'm asking You today to touch and heal me. By Your stripes, I am healed! Restore unto me the joy of the Lord." Then, you will be the voice of encouragement.

Empathize and put yourself in another person's place. Be sensitive and offer encouragement and inspiration. When you're experiencing pain and difficulty, the Lord will surround you with His word, His presence and people who will empathize and speak into your life. I know. I've experienced it!

ESSENTIALS

Ladies, do you leave the house to run errands and leave your purse at home? Your purse has all your essentials in it. It has your wallet, your keys, checkbook, cash, debit and charge cards, cell phone, and of course your lipstick! We would never leave our purse at home. Never!

One day I was in one of my favorite stores trying on shoes I didn't need. When I finished trying them on, I proceeded to look around the store a little more. When I got to the checkout counter, I realized I didn't have my purse! I ran back to the shoe department where I had been sitting, and there on the floor was my purse. It was right where I had left it. When I noticed I didn't have it with me I was in a state of panic! I already was thinking I was going to have to go get a new driver's license, call all my credit card companies, and of course I was thinking about the cash that was in my wallet. Oh ye of no faith!

Why do we often times lay the most important essentials in our Christian walk aside? Why do we just get up, walk off and leave them there? We often leave the most important things behind like prayer, meditation, fellowship with the Father, worship, and reading His Word – all the essentials we need to live a good Christian life. We lay those things aside and busy ourselves with nonessential things that dominate our time and leave us tired and exhausted. Some of these are even good things. But are they the commitments God wants us to make? Or, are we just busy and ignoring the most important things?

Hopefully, when we realize we've left all those important things behind, we'll run back to the place where we left them. Let's make sure we don't leave our essentials behind or neglect to pick them up. We need all of them to help us make it through each day. I was so focused on those shoes and how I wanted them, that I lost sight of the fact I would need some form of payment to be able to walk out of the store with them! What made me leave my purse there and just get up and walk off? I was distracted. I was focused on something else. So, what's distracting us? What are we so focused on that we would leave the most important things behind?

Lord, we come to you today and ask you to forgive us for losing our focus and leaving the essentials behind. We are running back to you, to the things that are important in life, and to serving you. In Jesus' name.

AWAKEN

Wake up everybody! Time to wake up. The act of awakening is to become suddenly aware of something. Shake off that slumbering spirit and get up! Get dressed! Get ready. God is about to take us places in the Spirit we've never been. Don't be lazy are lethargic. Don't pull those warm soft covers over your head and say, "Just give me a few more minutes!" No! It's time to get up and get moving. Don't hit the snooze button.

Can you feel it? Can you feel the change in the atmosphere? We are coming out of hibernation and out of a deep sleep. When a spiritual awakening occurs, we become aware of our surroundings. We are sensitive to what's going on around us. It may take us a minute, but eventually we become fully awake. Our senses are at an all-time high.

We become captivated and we can see clearly the path that is set before us.

We have awakened to an intense sensitivity – a sense of awe and childlike wonder. We have a new appreciation for life. Romans 13:11 MSG says, "Make sure that you don't get so absorbed and exhausted in taking care of all your day-by-day obligations that you lose track of time and doze off, oblivious to God."

Sometimes we're blinded to the needs of those around us. We need to wake up from our naps and be aware. The night is over. Dawn is breaking. It's a new day! Seize it. Make the best of it. Get up. Get dressed. Let your senses come alive and experience life. Do something you've never done. Be sensitive to the needs of others. Be captivated and experience the wonder of it all. Wake up! Appreciate life. Appreciate His favor and blessings. Crawl out from under those warm comfy blankets you've been buried under and experience life. Wake up!

FLAWSOME

If you are flawsome, you are awesome with flaws. And it's okay. Thank God we don't have to be perfect to be part of the Kingdom of God! Isn't that good to know? We aren't perfect. Everything in our lives is not going to be perfect. We have glitches, imperfections, and flaws.

I spent years trying to measure up. I tried to be the perfect daughter, mother, wife, pastor's wife, and friend. I guess you can say I tried to be everything to everybody. I tried to fix things and other people's lives until I realized it wasn't my job to be Sister Fix-It!

One day I realized Jesus was the only one I needed to please. That was so freeing! Just like the Scripture says in John 8:36, "He whom the Son sets free is free indeed." I was free to release myself from constantly striving to be everything to everybody. Free to set others free from expecting them to be perfect! I no longer had to demand perfection of myself, my friends, or my loved ones.

I realize how much God loves me, flaws and all. I realize He knew what my flaws and imperfections were, even before I did, but He loved me anyway. He still wanted me in His Kingdom, imperfections and all. How awesome is that? I was so excited to realize He accepts me and He just wants me to rest in Him and allow Him to work on all the areas of my life that need to be worked on. I could actually rest in Him and let God be God all by Himself!

None of us are without imperfections. We don't have to be hard on ourselves are take it out on others when we see imperfections in them. We just need to work on ourselves and let God take care of others. It's not our job to judge, criticize, or worry about others. We don't need to pull back from our calling or feel less than because we've made mistakes or wrong decisions. If anything, press in to God and move forward! Let's be determined to push through these areas as God perfects those things that concern us! I think we can all agree that He is working on all of us. We can help each other by just giving ourselves and others room to be... Flawsome!

STORMS

Wow! This storm came up quickly! It was so unexpected. We had just finished working in the yard and the sun was shining. We were sitting on the patio drinking a cup of coffee, admiring our clean manicured yard and all the hard work we had just completed. Then, out of nowhere (and I mean nowhere), these dark clouds rolled in and hovered. The wind began to blow, almost bowing over some of the large oak trees in our backyard. The lake water started looking like waves as the wind blew even harder and the water began to crash over the seawall. Then the rain started pouring. The winds were blowing dead, useless limbs all across the yard and suddenly our clean yard was full of debris!

I thought, well, I'll drink my coffee and just enjoy

listening to the rhythm of the falling rain. Then, a loud, deafening clap of thunder and horribly exaggerated lightning almost knocked me out of my seat. (Okay, I'm exaggerating a little.) I jumped up and ran inside, spilling my coffee. I almost felt like hiding under the bed with my cat!

Isn't that a picture of life? We are going along, everything is great and it seems like we have cleaned up the debris out of our hearts and minds. We seem to be moving forward, enjoying life and all of a sudden, a dark, threatening cloud appears, dissipating the sunshine and beauty of the day.

My mom was so afraid of storms. When she was growing up, if a storm came up, my grandfather would grab them and run to the storm cellar. She grew up with the fear of storms. In our house, when a storm came up, she would get so nervous and fearful. To counteract that, my dad would pick me up and start telling me how God created the thunder and lightning and how you could see God's handiwork and beauty in the storm. His calm spirit would calm both of us.

Friends, life is good when you're going along, you've cleared the debris, and the sun is shining. When the storms come in life, as they so often do, don't run and hide! Take shelter in Him, in the Word of God, and in worship. Let the winds blow, the thunder rumble, and the lightning flash. God is on the throne. Let your Father hold and comfort you in His arms, then you can see the beauty and wonder of the storm.

Storms are for a reason. They bring change in our lives and we learn how to go to our Father and allow Him to shelter us. We are always sheltered in the arms of God. The high winds blow out the debris in our lives that is dead and useless. The thunder serenades us. Lightning is a theatrical light show and the rain waters the dry parched ground bringing growth.

The storm eventually passed. The winds dissipated and the rain stopped. The thunder, I could barely hear echoing in the distance. That big, bad storm was gone! The sun was shining again!

CALM

Choose to live your life in a state of calm delight. God does not want us to live in dread or fear of the future. He does not want us to doubt our calling or destiny. He does not want us to reason or try to figure everything out. He doesn't want us to try to fix everything. That's not our job!

What He wants is for us to have peace that passes all understanding. He wants us to rest by the still waters and have joy unspeakable that is full of glory. He wants us to lie down in green pastures and for our souls to be restored. He wants our minds to be free of worry so we can have sweet sleep in the nighttime hours. He wants us to be reassured that He is working all things together for our good and for the good of those we love. He wants us to let go and let Him be God.

He wants us to know He is our ever-present help in time of need and that our past is forgiven. We can live free from guilt and condemnation. He wants us to not live in the past but to look forward to the future. He wants us to know He is the first and the last, the Alpha and Omega, our soon coming King. While He is perfecting those things that concern us, He wants us to chill out in His presence and enjoy abundant life. He wants us to stay calm.

THUMBS UP

Whose life can you touch today? Be aware of your surroundings and be sensitive to the needs of others around you. People need the Lord more than ever before. Life is just challenging sometimes, isn't it? People everywhere are hurting and going through the challenges of life.

Last year my son was in the hospital to have a procedure done and we were there a little longer than expected. As we were waiting, I went to the ladies' room where I encountered a lady crying and very upset. Her daughter was in surgery at that moment to have a nodule removed and the doctor had just informed her there was a possibility they would have to do a mastectomy. I asked her if she would like to pray and together we prayed and asked God for His presence and healing power to touch her daughter. We parted ways and I went back to the waiting room. About an hour later, she walked through where we were sitting with a huge smile and gave a big thumbs up. God had answered our prayer!

We just never know who we are going to cross paths with or when we'll need to be God's hand extended. We can always reach out to others, even though we ourselves may be in challenging circumstances ourselves. A thumbs up indicates something is very good. It's an expression of acceptance or agreement. We came into agreement in prayer for her daughter and we accepted that by Jesus' stripes she was healed. She walked through that waiting room with both thumbs up letting me know that the doctor's report was very good and that what we had agreed upon in prayer, God had answered!

TOUCH

Yesterday, I was visiting a friend in the hospital. I passed by the nurse's station where there was about six or seven nurses. They were all busy working, running back and forth. As I headed towards the elevator, the Holy Spirit said, "Go back and ask them if you can pray with them." I proceeded to tell the Lord why I shouldn't do that. "Lord, not right now. They are so busy. I can't interrupt them. What if they ignore me? This just isn't a good time. And what if..."

After the Holy Spirit won the argument, I walked back and said, "Excuse me ladies. Could I possibly pray with y'all?" They immediately jumped up, walked over, and without me saying anything they joined hands. I began to pray whatever the Holy Spirit dropped in my heart. When I said amen and looked up, tears were rolling down their faces. They thanked me and as I walked off I heard one of the nurses say, "That's the sweetest prayer I've ever heard. It touched my heart!"

Ladies and gents, it's time! It's time to walk out of our fears, insecurity, depression and discouragement and be His hand extended to a lost and dying world. People are stressed, hurting, tired, and feel hopeless. I was so surprised how quickly all of them jumped up, ran over, joined hands, and bowed their heads in reverence. People are ready to receive and ready to be encouraged and touched by the Spirit of God. People are desperate to cling to hope and to see something that is truly real. God is real and His Spirit is real!

No, I wasn't standing behind a pulpit, but God used me to minister to those who needed Him – those who wanted their hearts to be touched as one of the nurses expressed. God wants to use you in your circle of influence, wherever you are and whatever you may be personally going through. Bless others, serve others, be sensitive, be real, be available and when the Spirit of God says move, you move. When He says pray, you pray.

Oh to be His hand extended, reaching out to the

oppressed. Let me touch Him, let me touch Jesus, so that others may know and be blessed. Look around you. The fields are ripe and ready to be harvested. Let's all get our eyes off ourselves, stop feeding our insecurities, stop making excuses, and just let the Lord use you to touch others!

THE TOWEL

Have you ever heard the expression *throw in the towel*? It's a term normally used by boxers. When they throw the towel into the boxing ring, it's a sign of defeat. They are finished. They give up. It's over! When the boxer has suffered a beating, he throws in the towel. Now, just so you know, I don't watch boxing so I didn't know that. I googled it (just being real)!

You know, sometimes in life we feel like everything is an uphill battle. Have you ever felt like everything that could go wrong somehow does? You've been standing on the Word of God, confessing, declaring every scripture you know concerning what you're going through, and still no answers. You don't see anything and you don't feel anything. What I want you to understand is He's always working and He's always answering in His time. We have seasons in life where everything goes along great. The birds are singing, the sun is shining, the finances are great, health is good, children are great – everything is wonderful and life is good. Then, you wake up one morning and life happens. It's a different season – a season of challenges.

In 2000 we were going through the routine of life. Things were going well, we were celebrating a new year, and we had so much to look forward to. We had so many plans and we were excited about life. Then, the experience of life started.

In one year's time, my husband fell nine feet off a roof he was working on and broke multiple bones. Our home was broken into while we slept. Thieves went through every room in our house, opened the door to our bedroom and saw us sleeping. They thought no one was home, but we were there in a deep sleep. The sheriff commented, "You didn't hear anything? Boy, y'all were lucky. Most home invasions don't end well." Of course, we knew it was the hand of God that put us in a deep sleep so we wouldn't wake up and encounter the intruders. A few months later, my husband was diagnosed with prostate cancer and had surgery. All of this in one year! Did we feel beat up? Yes!

Did we feel like we were taking a beating and we just needed to throw in the towel, give up, and admit we were defeated? At times, yes. But God!

I encourage you today. Don't throw in the towel. Don't give up. Stay focused. Stay centered. Life truly is good – in the good times and in the bad. He's working all things together for our good! Aren't you glad? It is God's will, intention and purpose to bring about good for those who love Him. In other words, everything will work out! Just don't throw in the towel.

BRIDGE

Proverbs 4:10-14 is a scripture I feel is so relevant today for the older and younger generations.

> *Listen, my son, accept what I say, and the years of your life will be many. I instruct you in the way of wisdom and lead you along straight paths. When you walk, your steps will not be hampered; when you run, you will not stumble. Hold on to instruction, do not let it go; guard it well, for it is your life. Do not set foot on the path of the wicked or walk in the way of evildoers.*

I came to a place in my life where I began to embrace the changes God was trying to make in me such as surrendering my will and the way I thought things should be done, trying to force my opinion on others, and making the mistake of not listening to what others had to say. I wanted to continue to serve others and I wanted to be a ray of sunshine in a dark world, but I wanted to do it my way. Then, I began asking the Lord, "How can I serve You better? How can I make this transition into the next phase of my life and do it with class and dignity?" Well, don't ask if you don't want to hear what He has to say. Our Heavenly Father doesn't beat around the bush. He answered my prayers by showing me a new path, a new direction.

One of our associate pastors was speaking at a luncheon I was attending and he was motivating my generation to cross the generational bridge. As he was talking, I saw a mental picture of a bridge. My generation was standing on one side of the bridge and the millennial generation was standing on the other. There was such a wide distance between us. All of a sudden I realized my generation had to cross the bridge, take the millennials by the hand, and together we would cross into the future. It is together that we'll cross into the end times and into all God has for us – young and old.

If we as the older generation will respect, support, encourage, uphold and pray for this generation, there is no end to what we can do for the Kingdom of God together! It's exciting if you think about it. We can complement each other. We need this younger generation's fresh ideas. We need their energy, their strength and their enthusiasm for life. We need to be a part of their dreams and help them to accomplish them. They need our wisdom. They need to hear our testimonies of how we overcame the hardships of life and still stayed true to the Lord – holding our ground, winning our territory, being victorious and still standing strong. Are you ready? Let's cross that bridge and take the next generation by the hand into our future.

TURTLES

I absolutely love those *Millionaire* chocolate turtles. That's my go to, feel good, lift my spirits when I'm down treat. I have them stashed in secret places all over my house. That's right! I'm selfish with my turtles candy. I admit it!

As we get older, we sometimes entertain the thought that maybe it's time to just step back and let the younger generation step up. We start having thoughts that maybe we just need to take up playing bridge, oil painting, crafting or some hobby, and just enter rest mode. We put the voice of the Lord on mute and we stop listening to His voice as we think about what this phase of our lives will be like. It's time to unpause the pause button and unmute the sound of His voice so we can clearly hear Him.

I'll just be completely honest with you. I have, on more than one occasion, been guilty of listening to that negative voice telling me I'm not needed anymore. Maybe someone says something to you, offends you or hurts your feelings, and you just retreat into a shell of protection – protecting your feelings and walking away from the call of God on your life. When I gave in to those negative feelings, I found myself going to the secret place – not the secret place of the most high God but the secret places where I had my turtles stashed!

If you are over fifty-five, you are needed. You are desperately needed in the body of Christ. Don't listen to that negative voice trying to discourage you and make you feel useless. Use your gifting and calling to prepare the next generation. They need us and we need them. Learn to listen to that still small voice that gently leads and directs you. He will never whisper anything in your ear that will make you feel *less than*. He's a *more than* God! He wants you to know that by the grace of God, you can do more than you think you can! You are victorious and more than a conqueror at any age!

Come on! Let's go forward. I don't want to be guilty of

being stuck in the past in the good old days. Those were some awesome days and we should share with this generation the mighty works God did then, but we must not get stuck there. We must build this generation's faith and prepare them for the mighty works of God that will take place in the future.

Let's embrace new ways. God doesn't change but His methods will. All I know is that I want to be on the front row, right in the middle of everything. I want to embrace new ways, new ideas, and new technology. Let's give this generation our support and our prayers. I want to teach them the value of *Millionaires* chocolate turtles!

INVADE

Choose a word that speaks to your spirit today. As a matter of fact, ask the Holy Spirit to drop a word in your heart and then just have an encounter with the presence of God. Today He spoke the word *invade* to me. I just began to pray and ask the Holy Spirit to invade my space and fill it with His power, His glory, and His presence. Invade every circumstance, every situation, every challenge with Your wonder-working power. Invade my heart, mind, soul, and spirit. Change me. Change my attitude. Change my heart. Create within me a clean heart and renew a right spirit in me. Let Your Spirit overtake me.

Invade means to occupy, conquer, seize, or take over. It means to enter a situation intrusively. So go ahead, Holy Spirit. Conquer these areas of my life. Seize the areas that are out of control. Settle my spirit and bring peace that surpasses all human understanding. I welcome an intrusion of Your power into my family. Intrude on our plans and change them. Intrude in the lives of my children and grandchildren and help them keep their focus on You.

Invade also means to assail, assault, attack and take over. Do it! My ways are not Your ways and my thoughts are not Your thoughts. So please, take over! I've sometimes made a mess of things, trying to do it myself, trying to have all the answers, and failing to ask for Your help and guidance. I repent and I ask for Your forgiveness. Invade our lives! We need you! We need Your Spirit to take up residence in our hearts, bringing conviction back into our lives. Conviction is the ability to admit our sins and shortcomings. Lord, forgive us for lowering our standards and watering down Your word. We eagerly await the invasion of Your Holy Spirit!

BETTER

I want to surround myself with those who are better than myself. Those who are smarter, more talented, better speakers and better at doing life. I want to have friends I can learn from and grow older with. Those who will motivate me to be a better person. Whatever we need to do to be better, let's just do it!

I am willing to admit, I may not be as good at making homemade biscuits as you are, but I'm willing for you to teach me. I want to learn and experience new things. There are so many more adventures, more things to learn and new experiences to enjoy before I get a "new address." So, there is no need to compete with friends or family when we understand this concept and life lesson. If you want to be better, live and learn!

Let's be thankful that God has put these friends and family members in our lives. People who are impatient and aggressive can benefit from being around friends who are calm and patient. You guessed it! I'm the impatient one and I can tend to be aggressive. So, I'm so thankful for my laid-back, go with the flow, calm friends. You know who you are. God has used so many of my friends to teach and help me be a better person.

Let me tell you a story. When we first came to Word of Life, my home church, the pianist who was serving at the time was planning on retiring to Florida. I was going to step up and serve as the pianist when she made the transition. She began to require me to stretch, think outside the box, push me to be a better pianist, singer and musician. I mean, I already thought and had built up in my mind that I was the bomb! But, little did I know. She drove me crazy!

I was comfortable with how I was doing things and really didn't appreciate her input (just being real). Every emotion I had was tested. I mean, every emotion – anger, tears, feeling sorry for myself. "Why doesn't she like me?" "Who does she think she is?" "I don't have to put up with this. I can quit!" Well, praise God, she looked past my insecurities and immaturity and demanded a spirit of excellence! She chose to not give up on me, and to push me forward.

One night, about 15 minutes before service started, she walked out with an intro to a song. I still remember the song. It was *I Stand in Awe of You*. She instructed me to play it although I had never seen or practiced it before. I was so mad! As a matter of fact, it made me so mad that I dug my heels and I played the intro with the attitude, "I'll show you!" Afterwards, I took site-reading classes to better myself and my gift. I admired her confidence, her passion for life, and her passion for the things of God. I loved the fact that she was not a people pleaser. She was the real deal!

Now, I'm not a concert pianist, but I'm better than I was before she came into my life. She saw things in me that she knew she could help me with. She also saw attitudes that I needed to deal with to accomplish my dreams in life. She taught me many life lessons. She was and is a life coach before the term *life coach* existed.

If those who have degrees in music or singing and can teach me voice or theory, I want to learn. If I try to convince myself I'm as good a singer as you are and in reality I'm not, but want to get better, then I will allow you to teach me. I may never be on the same level as you, but I guarantee you this... I will be the best I can be and will welcome your instruction and input and I will have a blast while I'm learning! Go ahead girl! Speak into my life! I welcome it.

41188463R00062

Made in the USA
Middletown, DE
06 April 2019